Join my facebook coloring group and get a lot of free coloring books and coloring pages

IMPRESSUM / IMPRINT
Monsoon Publishing LLC
Email: info@monsoonpublishing.de
www.monsoonpublishing.de
facebook.com/monsoonpublishingllc
Gruppe: monsoon - malbücher für erwachsene

Monsoon Publishing LLC
www.monsoonpublishing.com
info@monsoonpublishing.com
facebook.com/monsoonpublishingusa
group: monsoon - coloring books for adults